FOR SAD GIRLS

FOR
MEETING ETTY HILLESUM
SAD
GIRLS

carolyn coman

namelos
South Hampton, New Hampshire

For bulk orders contact namelos llc
www.namelos.com
info@namelos.com

for Janet Shea and Susan Monsky
every step of the way

Contents

Sadness and Self

GIRLS OF ALL AGES LIE ACROSS THEIR BEDS AND
LOOK UP AT THE CEILING AND FEEL SO SAD THEY
WANT TO DIE.

I did—when I was twelve, when I was a teenager, and
later, at university, and afterwards, in my twenties,
when I was living with Han and the others in
Amsterdam. Even when so much of life was of interest
to me and filled to the brim, even after I met Julius
Spier and started therapy and took myself in hand,
there were still times when depression overwhelmed
me. Sometimes enough to want to kill myself.

If this happens to you, if you struggle, despite
enormous effort of will, to find consolation or relief
or meaning, you are not alone.

I have already—many years ago—recorded my life in
my diaries. But looking back is different from living
through. Looking back, I see connections I did not
see at the time, perhaps connecting even me and you.

If I tell, again, about the things that happened to me,
you need to understand that what mattered most were
not the external events but what happened within
myself. There was often little correlation between my
inner state and external circumstances. Perhaps that
is true for you sometimes as well.

Of course there were hard things that happened in my life that might explain the times of despair, just as there are hard things that have happened—or will happen—to you. We all have our temperaments and our circumstances, our ancestry and the sliver of history that our lives unfold in.

My life unfolded in Deventer and blossomed in Amsterdam during the Occupation and at Camp Westerbork, at a time when the world was eating itself alive.

Growing up, I had little enough to complain about, even if the home I was raised in sometimes felt more like an asylum to me. My mother's family was Russian, my father's Dutch. We were secular Jews, raised in a house filled with books and music—my younger brother Mischa was a child prodigy, an accomplished pianist by the age of seven. Both of my brothers and I were well educated, and my childhood was physically comfortable. My mother was erratic and my brothers high-strung; there was a lot of yelling. My father, the respected director of the local preparatory school, stayed largely outside the fray, his nose buried in a book. I took after him in that way.

There was mental illness in my family, and for a long time I harbored the fear that it was in me, too, a landmine set to detonate at any time. When we were both still young my brother Mischa suffered his first mental breakdown. He fled our respectable home on the corner of A. J. Duymaer van Twiststraat and lurched into the road as if he were on fire. Wailing. A neighbor returning from work jumped from her bicycle when she saw him, then joined my parents in their attempt to corral him. I remember watching from my upstairs bedroom window, completely separate and completely part of it at the same time. I remember the abandoned bicycle, twisted at an angle across our lovely tree-lined street, its front wheel still spinning. My parents and the neighbor formed a circle around Mischa and then tightened it, closing in as if my beautiful, fragile, adolescent brother were a rabid animal. In his wild state he must have thought they were demons descending on him. He held up his hands and stretched his arms out straight to ward them off. I remember the gesture, the almost electric energy emanating from his fingers—my brother the pianist, now a trapped animal, wailing. And I, behind glass, taking it all in.

Many years later—twelve, fourteen?—perhaps not so many years for some, but my world changed completely during that time—I stood behind another window and witnessed another level of human suffering altogether: men and women and children, two thousand of my people, packed inside the empty boxcars of a train for transport to Poland. I did not look away then, either, except to write it all down.

You may be thinking that your life does not contain a horror equal to mine. We are not in competition. I never believed that the suffering of one life or time eclipses the suffering of other lives and times. Prevailing circumstances are not absolute; they link to others, mine to yours, even.

My brother's illness was eventually diagnosed as schizophrenia; my other brother, Jaap, also suffered several episodes of mental breakdown that required hospitalization. Their suffering was real, as were my fears of our shared genetic makeup, but I cannot claim that they were the crushing weight that occasionally flattened me across my bed during those years when I was growing up, still living at home. Any more than my blazing Russian mother was, or the brushfire fights that tore through our home, or whatever boy or man I happened to be obsessed with who didn't care about me—didn't *think* about me—as much as I did about him. They were the circumstances of my life, then. Just as you have your own: think about them, whatever they may be.

The sadness that sometimes overwhelmed me as a young woman felt beyond circumstantial, though, and seemed to be mine alone—in me, of me. My brother could break my heart, and my family or boyfriends could make me want to tear my hair out, but my depressions had everything to do with me, and they constrained my life.

I never attempted suicide. I thought about it, but thinking—constantly, about almost everything—is what I did then: think, and talk, and fantasize, and ruminate. I used my journal, at least initially, to *record* my ruminations, and thoughts about suicide occasionally surfaced on those pages.

There were a few times, though, that the notion of killing myself sprang unbidden and fully formed into my mind: *Swerve your bike now, right into that oncoming car.* Those were the flashes that terrified me, that sprang from a deeper level of chaos than I was even conscious of, and that seemed a far more serious business to reckon with.

Once I began therapy with Julius Spier, I learned new ways to think about my depression. Spier (whom I variously called Spier, S., Herr Spier), said depressions were part of the creative process, not to be run away from or avoided. His rallying cry, "One must acknowledge one's pauses," became mine. He helped me see beyond the neurotic ledges I repeatedly stranded myself on. And he ushered me into a greater understanding of what it means to love.

I want to talk about love, and I will. I started off with sadness only because that's what set *my* course in motion. But is that not so for many girls? Sadness that always returns, sadness so great it pins you to your bed?

For a long time my only response to internal chaos was to take aspirin and crawl under the covers; the same remedy I used for menstrual cramps I used for psychic pain. I canceled appointments with the students I was supposed to tutor and burrowed deeper into my bed. The next day or the day after that, I'd emerge, feeling sheepish, and I'd resolve to never succumb again. I turned over many new leaves, a bushelful!

As part of my therapy with Spier I practiced a number of more practical, heartier techniques to rescue me from my descents: cold-water ablutions, brisk walks, even wrestling! They were stopgap measures, but they usually made me feel better, if only because I felt proud of having done *something*.

But I also began more long-term, serious, interior work that became my own small mission. There is an inner life and an outer life—I hope you understand that: there *is* an inner life!

As part of my inner work, I started writing. It had long been my deepest desire to become a writer. Facing up to true desire is not easy, and it took courage for me to begin. I did it in order to come to terms with my life. I wanted to become a truly mature human being. Writing in my diary helped me see my own tendencies and natural inclinations. I wrote down everything that was happening to me, inside me, and in doing so, wrote myself beyond it.

Discovering and traversing my inner life began with the intense scrutiny of what I thought of as my self—a topic of great and abiding interest to me, for which I make no apology! Nor should you, not if you harbor any hope of being free.

Know thyself: is that not a beautiful and essential command?

I was twenty-seven when I began my first serious reckoning with self, through therapy. Prior to that I relied almost entirely on books to speak to what was deepest in me. Dostoevsky, Rilke: they were my touchstones, and remained so, along with other authors I loved.

Spier had trained with Carl Jung in Zurich. He specialized in a particular field called psycho-chirology—the study of hands—an approach that in years to come would lose all claim to professional legitimacy. In his own time, Spier was a highly regarded therapist with a thriving practice, first in Berlin and then in Amsterdam.

Whatever doubts I sometimes entertained about studying palm prints in order to ascertain a person's tendencies and traits were ultimately quelled by seeing Spier at work. I was hardly alone in thinking that his mastery, or genius, stemmed from profound intuitive gifts. And as Spier used to say, hands were merely the way in.

What really mattered to me, of course, what I found irresistibly convincing, was that he helped me, over time, to overcome the tyranny of my moods. He brought me to a different understanding of myself by expanding my narrow mental horizon. It was Spier who encouraged me to keep a diary.

Han, my lover, often teased me about my interest in myself, the hours and hours I devoted to writing in my journal. *How can there possibly be so much to say about a single day? You write more than you live!* He wasn't wrong: I devoted some days to recording nearly every thought, filling one small black exercise book after another with my chicken-scratch scrawl. Developing the discipline to write honestly—and daily—was among the few revolutionary acts of my life. I won't apologize for it, or for the intense scrutiny of my inner life, or the mess much of it was, both to live through and to record. I got stronger learning about my weaknesses.

Even when Han would say with a bemused smile, *There's a whole wide world out there*, I didn't waver. Yes, there was a world out there, and it was bearing down on all of us and I was a part of it, looking to understand my place in it. Where else could I start but with myself? That seems such an obvious and valid question to me, and it was, of course, a basic premise of Spier's philosophy and therapy, although others surely saw it as self-indulgent.

I think Han misunderstood my desire to know myself, at least initially, as further proof of my egotism, as an end in itself. But I saw the work of becoming a mature human being as the necessary precondition for doing anything of real consequence in the world, for others. It was not for or about me alone. What I am saying is painfully obvious now, but when I was just starting out in therapy it was only painful and not at all obvious. And internalizing the things I discovered took time.

Early on in therapy I copied this line from a fable I liked: *Anyone who tackles an important task must forget himself.* I set the copied quote against the vase of flowers I always kept on my desk, to remind me where I was going and what I needed to do to get there. I understood that forgetting myself was the necessary condition for doing important work. And before I could forget myself I had to know who that self was! That's what I set my sights on, even if I didn't see clearly how that could be done or what exactly the work entailed. As for the *important task* that awaited me—what was it? I had only the vaguest notions. But, oh, the drive I felt to find out and to tackle it was enormous!

What is it that even makes something *important*? Do *you* know? On what basis do we decide? I was young, and I relied largely on my dreams and desires.

I wanted more than anything to write, to explore the world and record what I found there at the heart of things. I planned to travel to Russia and to make sense of that vastly different place and all it had to teach us. I harbored visions of bridging East and West. I never lacked for big dreams. And even when it became more and more apparent that my chance to live them out was doubtful, I still held them close.

Over time my bouts of depression diminished in both length and severity. I consigned less of my energy to sadness, and it lost its hold over me and took its proper, fruitful place in my life. Moments of despair did not evaporate entirely, but I came to see them as part of a natural and inevitable ebb and flow and trusted that I would always get the better of them. I drew from a source that never deserted me, and which I wandered from less and less. The inner life I discovered through therapy and writing and reading and prayer ushered me into rich territory more vast than any of my dreams.

MEN AND SEX

I RESIST ACKNOWLEDGING HOW MUCH OF MY LIFE I DEVOTED TO MEN. I bet many women could say the same. Honestly, though, doesn't it seem that often it is men, or being in love or unhappy because of them, that's at the root of what can feel so crushing? Looking to another for that which you can find only in yourself?

Imagine if there were a way to tally up all the time and all the thoughts you've ever given over to infatuation, to being in love, to the object of your desire, male or female. Don't you think the grand total might be shocking, something you might be inclined, out of pride, to deny or challenge? We want to be free, to be independent, we want to work and to passionately pursue our vocation, but we also long with all our heart for another.

It's not that I regret having loved the men I loved; I don't. It was the obsessing, the *wanting*, the always wanting *more, everything, all*—of them, from them. So many hours and days and months of my life given over to that; so much of the space inside me. That's how it was, though, there's no denying it. You can see for yourself how many pages of my diaries are consumed by them, even if, by the end, the emphasis had fundamentally shifted.

Here and now I would like to be honest about men, more honest than I sometimes was with them. I can give you a brief and partial history. So much of it is there for anyone to see, in my old diaries—all the infatuation and fantasizing and torment and analysis. I exposed myself a great deal in my journals, but that was the point. Considering it all in retrospect surprises me, although not for the reasons some others have found disturbing. I'm struck by the extent to which infatuation consumed me; others questioned my overlapping, boundary-less relationships, or the partners with whom I had them.

I was twenty-three and Han fifty-eight, a widower, when we became lovers. I'd answered his ad for a housekeeper—hardly my natural calling, but I was finished with university, uninterested in practicing the law I had studied, and open to anything. I moved into his lovely apartment on Gabriel Metsustraat, across from the Rijksmuseum, in the spring of 1939; we became lovers not long after. Han was a kind and even-keeled gentleman, a solid Social Democrat. I appreciated his calm, slightly bemused attitude toward life. I had energy and passion enough for us both; what I got from him was the steadiness that I lacked. Jealousy was really the only thing that disturbed his serene bearing. Then his posture became rigid and his eyes a little mean. I did my best to protect him from his jealousy, which is another way of saying that often I was not completely honest with him. I told myself that it was not important—or necessary, or kind—to tell Han everything I felt about and did with Spier, because it did not change how I felt about and what I did with Han. Often that was true. My affection for Han was deep and abiding. I sometimes joked that we were like an old married couple. Our arrangement suited us well, more or less, for years, right up until the day I left for the final time for Camp Westerbork, when he and my friend Maria stood in the road, tossing flowers until I was out of sight.

On February 3, 1941—a date I eventually declared to be my true birthday—Julius Spier entered my life. I was twenty-seven and Spier was fifty-four. My attraction to older men is not lost on me, but age difference mattered more to others than it ever did to me. Of course I read enough psychology and did enough therapy to realize that father issues were clearly indicated (Han's nickname was Pa Han!). But those "issues" were hardly the whole of my relationships, any more than psychology—or politics, or religion—can ever explain the whole of anything.

Spier was my therapist; I was also his assistant. He was charismatic and brilliant, my teacher and mentor; I was, for a long time, mad with desire for him, and on the rare occasion repulsed by him. Spier freely admitted—and acted upon—his attraction to me. His ability to flirt and occasionally dally with me and then return to business as if nothing had happened was a particular torture; I clung to our more intimate moments. But he was, above all, my teacher and friend.

He once referred to himself as a bridge for me to a great love, and I remember how crushing I found the notion. I did not want a bridge from him to anyone or anything else: I simply wanted *him*! I don't know how you would describe the way that you love, but when I loved someone—or even some thing—the depth of my desire was akin to greed.

So: I was in love with my therapist, who was engaged, by the way, to a woman in England; in love with a man twice my age who was still younger than my lover in whose home I lived. Can you construct an equivalent descriptive sentence about yourself, I wonder? And if you can, what do you make of it? Or can you simply not imagine it?

I will say this about my relationship with Spier: it was transformative. You can question the power dynamics between us, the age difference, the untamed egos. (I wanted to write simply *ego*—

singular, his. But we both struggled with our
egos—not to mention our libidos!) The relationship
was complicated. At its core, though, we shared a
genuine love and searching that brought me along,
that opened me to depth and dimensions I had not
known existed. He was, as he suggested, a bridge for
me. And it was in loving Spier that I finally moved
beyond the greedy, obsessive way of loving that had
been such a component of my misery.

Over two intense years my desire for Spier ebbed
and my love for him grew. My jealousy toward his
fiancée, Herta, dissolved. Ultimately I was ready to
let go of all my plans and dreams for us to remain
together, able to choose to go off by myself and do
what I had to do.

I hope you experience such a liberation someday,
too—not just from a particular person or relationship
that consumes you, but from the underlying
claustrophobia of romantic love. I can say from
experience, though, that liberation hardly feels freeing
in its early stages.

Before Han and Spier, I'd been with a number of men,
plenty of them, some even my own age. Max was my
grand, all-consuming passion while we were both at
university. I wanted him despite—or because of—his

being so unavailable: such a recipe for grand passion. But we were able, only a handful of years after the passion was spent, to walk arm in arm along the canals in Amsterdam, remembering our time together from what seemed like a great distance, and with fondness, as if a terrible storm had blown through us and much to our amazement left us standing.

I remained friends with all my lovers; there was never any reason not to.

My affair with Klaas Smelik—I was twenty-two; he was nearly forty, if you must know, now that I am bothering with ages—ended before I was with Han, and Spier, although every time I saw Klaas afterwards he reliably issued the invitation to renew it. (My friendship with his grown daughter, Johanna, turned out to be the more enriching relationship; isn't it so that deep friendships are what truly endure?) But when I was young and on the prowl, Klaas was irresistible: larger than life, a bon vivant, a writer—published by the same house that published my idol, Rilke! Imagine, *imagine*, the impression that made on me.

Klaas will forever round the bend in my mind in some sort of snappy vehicle, his cap cocked at a just-so angle. The first night I met him he was cooking perch he had just caught for a picnic by the river with his wife, Mien, and I joined them. So delicious, those fish! Later that same evening Klaas and I finagled some time alone. I remember his bright, appreciative eyes as I unbuttoned my blouse.

Years after our affair was over, Klaas tried, on two occasions, to kidnap me into safekeeping. I was steadfast in my refusal to go into hiding from the Nazis, and he in his refusal to accept my decision. He shouted that it was for my own good, my *survival*, as I kicked and squirmed to break free. For as much as I sometimes wanted to retreat from the world, I never, ever wanted to hide. I always said I would share the fate of my fellow Jews and could not be persuaded to exempt myself when others did not have that option.

Now that I've begun, I don't know that I have the energy to recount each and every relationship. My God, such drama! And so much longing accompanied everyone I slept with or wanted to—my fantasy life was vital and for years constituted a major part of my thinking—both men and women, singly or in pairs (I am remembering now the very real threesome with Spier and Dicky and me). And I am remembering my wrestling with Spier, that most tactile part of his therapeutic approach, all our rolling around on the floor of his office. Even when it did not turn explicitly sexual, sexual energy fueled it. We made complete fools of ourselves on more than one occasion.

I wonder what you make of your personal history— the one you most certainly have. Perhaps your tally of involvements includes more lovers, even greater abandon? Or maybe far more discretion and restraint? Maybe you're inclined to judge me. Others certainly have. But what others thought of me and how I conducted my life never mattered as much as my commitment to figuring out what I, myself, made of it and where it all was leading me.

I remember the exact moment I realized that my father and his colleague, Christine, were lovers: I saw him tenderly place a small Greek dictionary in her hands, and suddenly knew. And what was my response? I felt only happy for them, thankful for their mutual comfort and affection. I cannot see the point in judging others. Ask *yourself*: what sort of life are *you* leading, and are you who you want to be?

It's a formidable task to come to terms with the depth and breadth of our sexual desire and longing for love. Lumped together and separated from all else, my affairs paint a portrait of me that is incomplete, because despite the attention I gave them, they were not everything. Any more than *you* are simply the sum of your relationships and affairs.

The love I felt for men who came after I left Amsterdam for Camp Westerbork—for my dear comrade Jopie, and Osias Kormann, that good man, one of the camp's founding inmates, and Philip Mechanicus, the writer—all sprang from a heart that had been expanded. By then I'd come to see that I could not count on any one man or relationship to satisfy me, body and soul, and that love for all is more beautiful than love for just one.

And still, each romantic attachment I had held meaning for me, beyond just the sensual pleasure, which was sometimes there and sometimes disappointingly absent; sexual intimacy often produced an aching loneliness all its own, as if, having finally obtained exactly what I thought I wanted, I was left knowing that it was not, after all, enough.

We cannot talk about men and not talk about sex. And women, too, of course. I dreamed of women, fantasized about them; how I wanted to kiss Liesl's beautiful, medieval face! We cannot talk about *people* and not talk about sex!

For me, sexuality was a given: we have bodies, we *are* bodies ("Body and mind are one"; I can still hear Spier saying it).

I had a lover's body—I saw it every time I stood naked before the mirror. I used to splash my body with shockingly cold water in an attempt to wake myself up, inside and out, and then stand staring at my reflection. I appreciated that my body was capable of giving and receiving love, something I felt naturally constituted for. And when it came to loving, my body served me well. I used to say that I wouldn't last a month if I got sent to a labor camp, and I was not far wrong. First and foremost my body was an instrument of desire.

So, I was a lover, yes, but I was even more of a thinker. Spier used to point to my head and then to my heart and remind me that I needed to connect the two.

As much as I celebrated sex as a powerful and good force, it never existed in a vacuum for me. Inevitably there were layers and complications surrounding it. I sometimes had sex not because I wanted to, but because I could—in order to placate or make amends. Sexual as I was, my longed-for times of intimacy often led instead to a particular kind of emptiness, and confusing sex with intimacy always made me sad. Which isn't to say I wasn't an accomplished lover—I was! There were many moments of complete abandon and ecstasy, of course. But how rarely the physical pleasure eclipsed all else: the jealousies and mismatched longings and impossible expectations.

Jealousy, whenever it arose, was a poison. I am trying to think—was I ever jealous outside of relationships? Oh, I envied the slim ankles of the women who came to hear Spier lecture; I envied my friend Tide's sweet and pure singing voice. I envied Philip Mechanicus's travels to Russia. But envy is not the same as jealousy, and no, I did not really *suffer* jealousy except when it came to the man I wanted to be mine.

Despite my conviction that wanting to possess another was antithetical to love, despite Spier's and my many conversations about the idiocy of laying claim to someone else, jealousy was a current that flowed within my many intersecting relationships. Knowing better counted for next to nothing when faced with desire. It was a weight all its own in my history with men, or at least with Spier. In my other relationships, men were usually the jealous ones, but jealousy is a poison no matter which side it seeps in from.

How many times I faced off with Herta, Spier's fiancée, in the framed picture of her that he kept on the shelf above his bed. She, who could not speak from her framed altar, or hold or be with her beloved, and I, who could, and did. Of the three of us she was the one with the least, and yet there were times that I felt truly tortured by the sight of her smiling face.

There are portraits of me as well from that period in my romantic life—Han was an amateur photographer and often took my picture. One day he asked to photograph me when I was feeling absolutely consumed by my love for Spier. Never mind that I was posing for one lover engulfed by love for another—I stared longingly into Han's little black box of a camera, begging him to capture everything I was feeling; I wanted to see for myself what Grand Love looked like. Suddenly Han stopped snapping pictures and raised his head. Irritated and a bit bewildered, he told me: *Don't be pulling faces.* Whatever my expression was in the instant that his words registered: I think *that* might have been a true portrait of me.

How do we learn what being faithful means? To whom or what do we give ourselves without reservation? I struggled with these questions, just as you might. Writing honestly about them in my diary was as honest as I could be until the answers emerged and settled inside me.

I am not telling you any of this by way of confession; I am only looking back and saying what I see, the same work I did from less distance in my diaries, at the time it was all happening. There were romantic relationships that preoccupied me. But relationships were also the messy means through which I learned a great deal about love and faithfulness and even about greater intimacies.

Eventually both internal and external forces had their way with me; my inner life deepened and history intervened.

No doubt you have your own complicated involvements—or lack of them—and perhaps they weigh on you, too, as mine did on me, occupying more space in both heart and mind than you would wish. I'm sorry if you have tortured relationships you feel you can't break free of, or attractions that seem to endlessly get the better of you. These kinds of struggles are so easy to dismiss as self-involved, immature. But I know just how real and hard they are, and I know that how you reckon with them can bring you to a greater understanding of yourself and of suffering.

Marriage and Children, or Not

As REMOVED AS I WANTED TO BE FROM ANSWERING TO CONVENTIONAL DEMANDS ON MY LIFE, I was hardly beyond the expectations and pulls of family, society, and tradition.

I did not want to ever get married.

I *dreamed* of getting married.

I wanted to marry Spier.

But only so we might stay together if we were rounded up by the Nazis.

Or so I told myself.

I wanted to live on my own, unbeholden.

I wanted to be a writer more than I wanted to get married.

I thrilled to the ideals of independence and sexual freedom, even as I daydreamed—and I often did—of marriage, of one great, lifelong love, *you alone forevermore*. It was so much easier for me to keep my distance from other institutions—organized religion, political parties. When it came to marriage, I wavered, I struggled, I played out all sorts of fantasies.

Spier fled Berlin to escape the Nazis, but even after he was legally living in Amsterdam, the Gestapo there continued to hound him, demanding that he turn over any remaining articles of value that he had brought with him. One day he sent me off with a collection of things to appease the thieves at the bank. The collection included his old wedding ring, from his marriage that had ended in divorce. I couldn't help myself—I took it out and put it on, so big I wore it on my thumb as I walked along, debating once again whether I really wanted to marry the man. Not that he had asked! I think on that particular occasion I decided he was too old and I was too determined to travel on my own and write, but there were so many times of torturing myself about it, planning how we could stay together if the Nazis rounded us all up and put us in camps. I was sincere in my desire to stay together and help him in any way I could, but I was also infatuated, and marriage invariably appeared as infatuation's inevitable destination in my furrowed thoughts.

Why wouldn't it? I was surrounded by marriage. Aren't we all? It was almost as much a given in my life as being Jewish, being Dutch, being a woman. Whenever I left Amsterdam to visit my parents in Deventer I always heard the news—who, among my old friends and classmates, had married, had had children. It was a race I had to remind myself I did not necessarily have to run.

Spier's marriage had ended in divorce before I met him. Han was a widower. My married friends closest to my age were Liesl and Werner, pillars of culture and education, a beautiful couple with two beautiful children. Liesl always said that life without Werner and the girls was absolutely inconceivable to her, even as I knew she no longer wanted to have sex with her husband, who always wanted sex. Her solemn, sad face sometimes revealed the misery she felt. No arrangement—no pairing, no not-pairing—is without its problems.

My parents' marriage lasted thirty years before they were murdered. Theirs was a mismatch of grand proportions, a disaster. They did not belong together, and they stayed together. I never wanted what they had. I also came to see that I underestimated what they had. After my parents were brought to Westerbork I watched my proud mother string a line between the bunk beds of an overcrowded barracks and then hang my father's washed handkerchiefs to dry, utterly given over to what I could finally see as an act of love. The quotidian in that place of such suffering sometimes blindsided me; how much more people were capable of bearing than I'd given them credit for.

One day in the camp I came upon a beleaguered gathering in the barracks where I'd gone to visit the writer Philip Mechanicus. In the center of the circle stood an ancient man and his tiny wife, and beside them their grown son, calling down blessings upon them on the occasion of their sixty years of marriage. The old man leaned down to kiss his wife, and all the prisoners gathered around them clapped. I, too, applauded, despite or because of or beyond the horrid setting and circumstance, knowing nothing of their union but its longevity and its likely imminent ending.

By then I had begun to know more about the many forces that bring people together and keep them together or separate them, and how little all our plans sometimes count for. Marrying or not marrying—for a time in my life it seemed a decision that needed to be made and which would make a very big difference in how my life proceeded. And then it all but vanished from my concerns. And as for having children, I knew I would not.

When I was twenty-seven, I became pregnant. I'd been living with Han for four years. I'd endured a number of false pregnancy scares prior to that, but in December of 1941, my luck ran out. What a torture my menstrual cycle always was, whether I got my period or not.

I never doubted for one minute that I would terminate
the pregnancy. It was my choice to make, and I made
it, and once it was finally over I had no regrets. I
did what I had to do, I did everything that I knew
or had heard whispered to do, and after a week
or so of scalding baths, and copious amounts of
quinine water, and prodding about inside myself
with various instruments that make me cringe to
remember, I had a self-induced abortion. Käthe,
our dear German cook, looked after me; Han was
concerned and sympathetic from a remove. He had,
already, four adult children from his marriage; when
he and I became lovers it was certainly never with the
intention of starting a family.

The pregnancy and its termination tested something
I had always assumed about myself, and helped
me know it for sure: that I did not want—was not
meant—to be a mother.

When I was at Westerbork, I participated in a rescue
operation to sneak children out of the camp in order
to save their lives. (I wanted for them what I refused
to consider for myself: escape.) I believe I also saved a
life in terminating my pregnancy.

I could not conceive of passing on genes that might
send a child wailing into the road like a hurt animal,

or into a world threatening her extinction. Perhaps you feel the same way about your world, now, and perhaps you are right. The world has been called inhospitable at every point in history, undoubtedly, and not without cause. There were compelling external reasons to end the pregnancy. Even more compelling, to me, were the interior ones having to do with my temperament, my sense that I was destined for other things altogether.

My mother had three children, had us and suffered with and for us (and, at times, made us suffer!). My mother, who is often blamed for the act that resulted in her and her family—Papa, Mischa, and me—being put on transit, did what she did in a misguided act of mother love, of trying to protect her son. I had great love in me, too, but I did not want a child of my own.

I did not want to be a mother, but there were children in my life. In Amsterdam, Werner and Liesl's daughters, Renate and Mirjam, were always racing through the flat when I visited my friends, climbing up their father like he was a jungle gym. I was with them all the night we had to wear our yellow stars for the first time. The girls played, the adults drank dark, delicious, impossible-to-find coffee and talked about who among us would survive in a camp. We had no idea, then, what a camp might even look like, even though Westerbork was only 130 kilometers from where we sat.

Weeks later, I walked with Liesl and Mirjam, lugging old coats and woolens to the dressmakers to be made into more functional clothing; by then we were preparing for the call-ups that were rumored to begin soon. Signs all around us proclaimed NO JEWS—at the park, in the doorways of nearly all the shops. It was springtime and I had spring fever. I remember wanting to kiss Liesl, take her beautiful face in my hands and kiss her lips. After we dropped off our clothes, we walked to the Jewish Quarter and found an ice cream store where we could be served. I watched as Liesl gave Mirjam all the time in the world to make her agonized choice of which flavor to have. I felt the cable that ran between the two of them as Liesl cupped her daughter's face in her hands. I loved them and I knew: I will never have children.

I was already at Westerbork, hoping never to see Renate and Mirjam at that place, when they arrived, wide-eyed and stunned in their parents' arms.

I once confided to my dear friend and comrade Jopie my deepest desire: that I would be spared having to witness my own family's suffering at Westerbork. I knew by then how much more I was able to give of myself to others absent my family's presence. Of course, I was not spared; it was hardly a sparing time. But Jopie, whose wife and two children were with him at the camp, said they were the *source* of his strength and hope. His third child was born there. I held him when he was just days old.

There were many children at Westerbork. My compatriots were able to sneak out only a very small number of them from the camp, and I lived among the thousands who passed through.

Once the weekly transports from Westerbork began, I worked through endless nights in hell, helping to dress babies and toddlers, tending manic mothers or those paralyzed by the impending departure, those who cried out to their God again and again, asking how he could allow such a travesty. I knew no such God. I knew that our own human hatred had brought us to where we were.

One night a boy who had been listed for transport the next day ran away and hid. They found him eventually, but by then the commandant had already added fifty more to the list in retaliation for his action. I thought about that boy long after he had been found and loaded into the train car, some mother's child, and how it would go for him there.

Children played nearby on the early morning that I sat with my friend Philip Mechanicus to witness and chronicle the departure of the weekly transit. As the train filled with its load of human cargo, the little ones continued on with their games, taunting one another, changing and bargaining over the rules of their make-believe. Occasionally, though, they took breaks to stand at the window with us and observe what could not possibly be taken in.

Everyone bore so much, each in their own way. You are bearing whatever burdens are yours. We have extraordinary capacity within us.

Murder foreshortened my life. I did not get to decide, finally, whether I would marry or not, or to discover if anything might have changed how I felt about having children of my own. However you feel about marriage, about having children, whatever decisions you make or are made for you by circumstances you cannot foresee, the fact remains that there *are* children. And they are the ones, if *they* survive, who inherit the world we leave them.

Proceeding

I wanted to know, more than anything, how to live my life: how to fathom the depths of my soul—is that a word you are comfortable with? I always was—and then live accordingly in good faith. Figuring all that out was not an idle concern or a strictly intellectual proposition. For me, it was a matter of life or death—freedom if I could answer to what was deepest within me and death if I couldn't—which is why I devoted myself to it so relentlessly. It became unthinkable to me that I would live an accidental life.

Do you know who you want to become? Do you know where, and in what, you find meaning? Or maybe that is not a question you even wonder about. Perhaps you don't believe that anything at all has meaning. Then it is hard to hold on to life.

I held on to a number of lifelines.

Relationships were crucial, even as my under-standing of them changed over time. For much of my life I lived in an ever-expanding whirl of friendships and romances, connections of all kinds, all of which I considered important and fascinating, and which I exhausted myself trying to maintain. Eventually, as is only fitting, the accidental ones fell

away. At Westerbork I developed friendships enough
for several lifetimes.

As I matured I spent less time trying to be interesting.
I learned to carry people inside me, so that it did not
matter where our bodies were. I loved more broadly.
Bonds, not chains: that's what I aspired to—and failed
at, often enough—in my relationships. Ultimately
we are alone with all our experiences; they are ours
to belong to and to transform, just as Rilke said. But
relationships were a sustaining part of my life. They
clarified my relationship with God and all of humanity.

Philosophy, psychology, religions—disciplines that
order and make sense of the world from a certain
perspective, that even offer directives for how to
respond to and live in it—all of them, to varying
degrees, taught me. But as much as I craved a single
system, or a perfect formula for how to live, I did not
find one that on its own was enough.

Literature, music, and art were fundamental sources
for me. The small act of copying wise words from the
books that nourished me—poems, paragraphs, entire
pages—was an abiding source of comfort.

Ideas thrilled me; I'll admit that I was intellectually
greedy. Our whole little group of students and

musicians and professionals—how pleased we all
were with our active minds! But intellect is so sure
of itself and so often charged with ego. My brother
Jaap once mockingly wrote to me in a letter: *I think,
therefore I am; you believe, therefore you are not.*
Thinking has its place, but it's hardly everything.
Honestly, much of my thinking was nothing more
than brooding, and many of my thoughts became
millstones. How many of your thoughts, the contents
of your mind, constitute real insight or nourishment?

I remember Klaas, stalwart Trotskyite that he was,
confessing to me once in an unguarded moment: *I'm
filled with despair. I don't know what to believe in.*
It was a rare moment of vulnerability, precious for
me to witness in a man usually so sure he had all the
answers. But we all come to crossroads that present
us with essential questions of how and on what basis
we will carry on.

When it came to my refusal to hide from the Nazis,
Klaas despaired of what he called my naïveté. I could
never make him understand that I felt beyond the
Nazis' clutches because I felt essentially free. I breathed
unrationed air; I harbored increasingly unassailable
inner resources; I refused to partner with anyone's
attempt to humiliate me. I insisted that rooting out
every last atom of hatred in ourselves was the essential

work to be done, the only work that would ultimately make any difference in the world. "But that's nothing but Christianity," he sputtered in disbelief. (Actually, he was trying to kidnap me into hiding at the time.) "And what's wrong with that?" I answered him. Many of Christianity's teachings were dear to my heart, just as my identity as a Jew was solid, indisputable.

Yes, I was a proud Jew, and for the most part proudly irreligious. (I say that, and yet there were times I admitted that deep down I *was* religious—an ambivalence that stems from what *religious* even means.) I went through a phase as a teenager when I joined a Zionist group and participated in various classes, but that immersion was not unlike my later involvement in political groups and protests when I was at university. Both held my interest for a time, both spoke to and shaped certain beliefs, but neither held me in their grip. I found more in literature, in poetry, in sitting in silence in the sun peeling potatoes than I ever found in a synagogue, or at a political rally, at a service of any kind.

My friend Werner wanted me to be a more devout Jew. One of the students I tutored in Russian harbored hope he might make me a Christian. (I finally disabused him of the notion by declaring my conviction that no afterlife awaited us.) I remember a gathering I attended one night—when such gatherings were still permitted—at Werner and Liesl's flat: an open discussion between Spier and Werner on Christianity and Judaism. Werner, ardent Zionist, spoke passionately for Judaism, and Spier, also a Jew, spoke on behalf of Jesus (a role he seemed quite comfortable with). Their arguments, articulate and sharp, made for a stimulating evening, just as they were intended to. But scoring intellectual points in an argument about religion felt, to me, so many steps removed from the heart of the matter.

I did, despite my declared irreligiosity, come around to reading the Bible. It was a revelation of sorts to realize that Spier read the Bible the way that I read Dostoevsky or Rilke. It spoke to his soul the way that poets and great writers—especially the Russian ones—spoke to mine. Gradually I came to see how rugged and thrilling the Bible is, Old Testament and New, both. It was among the first things I packed to take with me to Westerbork, and what I opened to a random page as I sat on transport. Certain passages became bedrock in my life:

> *And what good is it all if I have not love?*
> *Do whatever your hands find to do and do not take thought for the morrow.*
> *We are made in the image and likeness of God.*

How much more those words spoke to me than any proclaimed dogma ever could. Does dogma truly satisfy anyone?

At university, politics was pervasive, setting us all on fire, especially as things grew worse and worse—teachers dismissed, or rounded up and thrown into prison. We talked and raged, held passionate debates late into the night. I was a young woman living in an eclectic household in Amsterdam, surrounded by Marxists, Communists, Social Democrats, members of the Resistance, Christians, atheists, agnostics, Jews, even some irritating theosophists. All my friends were political, and I was, too, although unlike some of them I could never wholeheartedly embrace any set ideology: Communism. Socialism. Nationalism. I was not drawn to answers that created more divisions, or to organizations endlessly staking their claims. At some point all systems become systemically infected; fear and hatred of others invariably creep in.

Indiscriminate hatred is the worst thing there is—
I wrote that a long time ago, in my diary. And lived to see how terribly that truth bore itself out. At Westerbork I studied the faces of those who brutally loaded the transports with the sick and elderly, the face—many called it handsome—of our

commandant, moments before he imperiously sent a trainload of people off to their deaths. They were faces utterly devoid of human warmth, impossible for me to read and among the few things that ever genuinely frightened me.

Of course, it's easy enough to see hatred in others; then comes the awful moment you have to address it in yourself. Nothing can fundamentally change as long as I harbor hatred, or as long as you do: that's what I came to believe.

There were times when I could almost taste it—the deliciousness of a hatred so righteous and well-earned as toward the Nazis. The invitation came often enough, a fitting crescendo to news of the latest outrage. *Bastards*: I savored the sound of the word in my mouth, perfectly bitter. I joined in one late-night session, calling out for those bastards to suffer for what they were doing to us, to ours, while Käthe, our German cook, worked within earshot, in the kitchen—a good woman hurt so I could taste my morsel of self-righteous anger. The realization that personal bitterness was unequal to the magnitude of the evil we were confronting eventually took root in me; I came to see that if you don't hate, the desire for vindication and revenge never arises.

Please don't think me stupid or blind to what was happening around me, to the evil of the actions and the insidious thinking that justified them. I was fully aware. But that expansive stretch into blaming an entire people—I remember how hopeless I felt hearing my friend say that given the chance he would happily kill every German he could—*every last one*. By then it was already dawning on me that we need to destroy in ourselves what we think we ought to destroy in others.

I spent a good amount of time analyzing myself and analyzing others. Psychology was a natural fit for me. I always wanted to understand why people behaved the way they did; I felt it was my task to decipher them. I once infuriated a young German soldier by failing to be frightened by his attempts to intimidate me. But more than anything I was *curious*: what had brought him to who he had become, to his bullying way of behaving? Who had intimidated *him*?

It was much the same when a man at the pharmacy became enraged that I, a Jew, had the audacity to think I was within my rights to purchase a toothbrush. What astonished me—and the mystery I most wanted to plumb—was why and from what his *need* to humiliate and exclude had arisen.

Psychology was also helpful in understanding much of what blocked me, and what blocks most people—family history, complexes, unconscious urges. As clarifying as psychological insights often are, though, I never believed that they were some sort of ultimate explanation for everything. Therapy cleared the path for deeper, more encompassing work.

There is a German word, *hineinhorchen,* that is difficult to translate, but refers to deep, interior listening. It comes as close as any to describing what ushered me further into the inner landscape—a harkening to your true self that is vitally connected to what is deep and true in others. I remember accompanying Spier to the doctor once, when his lungs were first beginning to trouble him. With the bell of his stethoscope pressed to Spier's heart, the doctor stood utterly still, at complete attention, fully listening. *That,* I thought—*that* might come close to capturing *hineinhorchen*: what is essential in one, harkening to what is deepest in another. What I am talking about is not unrelated to prayer.

Spier was the first person I knew who knelt by his bed and prayed every night before he went to sleep. Such an exotic thing to do! I often wondered what he said, what his prayers consisted of, but I could never bring myself to ask—I who questioned him about everything under the sun. But I intuitively understood how deeply intimate prayer is.

Eventually I, the self-proclaimed *girl who could not kneel*, learned to kneel, too—on the rough coconut mat in our little bathroom! It didn't seem exotic so much as a bit awkward at first, just as it is awkward now, trying to convey this gravity-like force that brought me to my knees. Nothing in my upbringing or ancestry foretold it. But over time kneeling became a natural gesture and prayer a sustaining part of my life, whether I was kneeling or not, part of a constant dialogue.

Do you want to know what my prayers were, just as I once wondered about Spier's most intimate communication? Sometimes prayers rose up in me unbidden and I called them out to the night as I pedaled home on my bicycle. Some I confided to my diaries. I gave thanks for beauty and for never losing sight of it: for being able to see it in the midst of all else. I prayed to become more simple and I prayed that people, all of us, be able to bear what there is to bear. I sought and found deep reserves of inner strength. Petitioning for favors—relief from my sadness, or happy outcomes, or fixes for the broken world we were living in—never made any sense to me. The God I prayed to is not responsible for whatever human conditions we create. If anything, the God I prayed to needs *our* help—and is that not a reason to live?

Prayer became a protective wall around me, and in turn I became God's guardian. Prayer was a refuge but never an escape from external realities. I loved our world in all its beauty and all its horror, hardly immune to its madness.

I discovered that there was always a quiet corner to be found in some part of my being—just as there is in you. Prayer was often the most important part of a day, a turning inward that nourished and replenished me. The unexpected sources of silence, listening, and prayer all came to me and took hold. A deeper inner life opened to me and I surrendered to it.

Sometimes I felt like I ricocheted back and forth between what I came to experience as the timelessness of the inner life and the undeniable, time-bound realities of circumstances and the growing calamities of fascism. Finding the balance between inner and outer reality is not easy, or it wasn't for me. I had to work at it. But outer reality became less and less able to inflict real damage on me as I grew stronger. Over time I came to see that my real life took place within, regardless of external circumstances, even as I tried to be entirely present in those circumstances. Truly, I embraced a new reality.

There were moments when I was convinced that what I wanted was complete solitude, utter renunciation of all worldly things. But the truth is that I lived in the world and I loved it. I was so deeply connected to people, naturally constituted to loving them. I yearned to travel, to speak many languages, to write about everything I saw. I was not immune from— nor did I want to be—what the world was up to, all it was handing me and my loved ones, my country, my people, the present moment that was constantly feeding history. In one of the first prayers that rose up inside me, unbidden, what I called out was my desire to find God in others, in everyone in the world— hardly the wishes of someone destined to be a recluse.

I told you that I wanted to become a mature human being. I wanted to live a proper life (and surely you understand I do not mean by that prim or proscribed), and I wanted to live it faithfully. I followed an unlikely path in finding my way, but enlightened moments gradually reshaped my everyday life; prayer merged with action. I gauged my progress by whether I was growing in strength and developing a steadily increasing inner concentration.

I am telling you these things about myself so that
if you are desperate not to feel as despairing as I
sometimes did, you will consider what there is for
you to hold on to and what life-saving work you
can do to take yourself in hand. There is no one set
formula or answer. We have to find our way, and we
stumble along whatever path we're on, of course we
do; we have lapses, our hearts fail us at times. But ask
yourself, what do you want your life to be? What is
there to be done that is worth doing? What do you
hold within yourself that you can return to, again and
again, and be renewed?

I have no doubt it was interior work that prepared
me for and guided me through the external
circumstances I ended up experiencing. Inner work
changed me—how I felt and reacted, how I saw the
world and my place in it. I was very rarely ever afraid.
With practice I found myself calmed and renewed by
even short periods of recollection, by a few chosen
words from poet or prophet, able to embrace life's
contradictions and return to the exploding world
around me and still find it beautiful.

WORK AND WRITING

MY VOCATION WAS WRITING, BUT I HAD VARIOUS
KINDS OF WORK EXPERIENCE: student of law,
student and tutor of languages; housekeeper and
general overseer of our ecumenical household on
Gabriel Metsustraat; budding psychologist. For
several weeks before I asked to be reassigned to
Westerbork, and for approximately a year after
I arrived there, I was an employee of the Jewish
Council. At the camp I worked for the department
of "Social Welfare for People in Transit." My job
allowed me to help many people in many ways; it
also afforded me certain privileges others did not
have, and ultimately the council served the Nazis'
agenda: conflicts that I reckoned with. In the end, the
council was disbanded and we workers were declared
prisoners, and I took my place among those with
whom I had chosen to be, to face our fate together.

But no matter where I was and what else I was doing,
I always wanted to write. Over time, as I kept my
diaries and wrote letters and documented life at
Westerbork, I discovered how much recording life, in
one way or another, mattered to me. I couldn't *not*
write. The threat of pen and paper being taken from
me was one of the few things I truly feared. Even
when we were packed like cattle on the train, leaving
Westerbork on transport, I wrote a card to my friend
Christine van Nooten and threw it from the window. I

told her the Bible passage I had opened to: *The Lord is my high tower.* I told her, *We left singing.*

You may not yet know your vocation, the important work that awaits you, but the desire to do it is in you, and you are running toward it or away from it, circling around it, giving yourself hints every which way you turn.

My passion for books was so telling. Is it possible, I wonder, for someone to love books as much as I did and not harbor the desire to write? My brother Jaap accused me once of living my life like a character in a book, and I didn't take the offense I'm sure he intended. In fact, I rather liked the notion; I sometimes thought of my life as a book in the making. When I tried to capture the magnitude of all that I was learning from Spier, I described him as a book I would read forever. And in all my ruminations about what I would bring with me were I to be called up, it was always books that I considered first. Books were, in fact, the treasure I took with me to Westerbork, and then, later, on transport: my Bible, the Koran, Dostoevsky, Rilke.

And then there are the "books" that I wrote, the tally of my life's labor: eleven small black notebooks—my diaries—barely legible, written between 1941 and

1942, mostly at the desk in my room at Gabriel
Metsustraat, my beloved sanctuary; I wrote a great
many letters as well—to Spier, to friends, to clients,
my reports from Westerbork. Some were saved, some
lost. In the end, I did not write all that much.

Of course the tally does not include the books
I wanted to write, planned to write, might have
written. My novel: *The Girl Who Learned to Kneel*.
My dispatches from Russia if I ever made my way
there after the war. My treatise on men and women.
I had dreams, I had plans. I wanted to write the
biographies of a thousand different lives. I wanted to
record the history that was destined to be left out of
history books, about the men and women who kept
God alive through terrible times, who shared their
food or at least didn't sell it at black-market prices;
the man who voluntarily put himself on transport as
a final act of agency.

Who knows what I would have pursued had my life
continued. For a while I thought I would become
a therapist after the war, or a writer who traveled
far and wide to report on the world. I did not lack
ambition, that ridiculous thing.

My diaries and letters may not constitute a towering
body of work, but they are mine, of me, and I stand

behind them. The level of self-consciousness in them can be overwhelming, I know that, especially in many of the early entries. Even as I wrote them I sometimes castigated myself for my lofty notions and sophomoric profundities, but I was trying, as best I could, to tell the truth about what I was thinking and feeling, and to make sense of both inner and outer realities. They show the stuttered progress of my true self being forged. How could I disown my attempt, through words, to come to an understanding of myself and my world, the witnessing of my own transformation?

I hope you honor whatever record of your life you may have kept, or be keeping, or be soon to begin. Find your form. Take yourself and your work, whatever it is, seriously.

For myself, it was all a matter of looking for the right words: I said as much early on in my diary, and that is what it came down to. But what a rocky path I took toward simplicity. Spier told me I "toyed" with my talent, and I did. (I also toyed with men, until the day came that I knew it had to stop; I had grown beyond it.) It took real practice for me to become a true reader and not just an obsessive one. When it came to my writing, I suffered with procrastination and the scourge of wanting things to be perfect. Maybe it's the same for you. I despaired of ever knowing what my material would be, despaired of the gulf between what I imagined and what I actually produced. I struggled with staying focused, giving work concentrated attention. There were so many times that I felt I was just slogging through, unable to clearly express what I meant. Well, slogging is part of the process, too.

Can I remind you, as I had to remind myself over and over again, of the need for patience—in whatever it is that constitutes our work, in our growth, in our reckoning with depression and sadness and grief? Spier always said that development knows no time; Rilke said that patience is all. I repeated those maxims to myself again and again, my mantras.

Have you read Rilke's homage to the artist Rodin? He so admired Rodin's discipline, his "profound concentration for the form's sake." We all need models of how to work, how to answer to the process—the habit of it, the perspective from which we approach it. I hope you have teachers who can show you the way to enter and enact your work. If you don't, find them. I learned so much from Spier. He taught me the importance of following through. If I didn't, he told me, my soul would bear what in my body would be scars. And he showed me *how* to work even more than what work to do: the hour-by-hour, day-by-day steadfast doing of it. He also made clear what guided him. When I thanked him once for the kindness with which he had responded to my brother Mischa, he told me, "You cannot heal disturbed people without love."

The work that is yours to do with love will come to you, and all the different things you've done before then—however menial or seemingly unrelated to your true vocation—will have prepared you in some way.

Writing my diaries nurtured discipline and commitment in me. They captured a particular period in my life and a particular moment in history, even though a historical record is not what I was after, at least initially. I had to get to the bottom of myself first. External developments never held my interest the way interior ones did; I believe that how we see things is a reflection of our inner landscape.

In the first year of keeping a diary I was far too preoccupied with my depressions, my love life, my need to understand how my mind and heart worked, to pay much attention to the outside world. I rarely recorded the particulars of political developments. Certainly the Occupation inflicted its discontent and worries, but in the beginning it affected my day-to-day life only slightly. I was more troubled by my psychological state than I was by seeing German soldiers on the street—boys who looked homesick to me and whom I found it impossible to hate.

When history finally flooded my life, it intersected with the center that I had discovered deep within me. My desire to chronicle my time, from the inside out, increased. The opportunity to document a slice of history presented itself to me, and I was open to it.

Leaving Amsterdam for Westerbork forced an early reckoning in me about what to do with my diaries. I could have destroyed them, but I decided not to. Instead, I gathered them together and gave them to my friend Maria Tuinzing for safekeeping. I instructed her to turn them over, if I did not return, to my favorite scoundrel, Klaas Smelik, who I thought would be in a position (if *he* survived) to have them published. I wanted that. What woman who dreams of being a writer does not want her work published? Such an odd position to find myself in: knowing that the publication of my journals would mark not only the naked exposure of my life, but also my death. At least, I told myself, I would be spared whatever harsh criticism my outpourings might inspire.

At Westerbork, my writing clarified and simplified.

Moving toward our destruction focused me. I had changed, and so had what there was to see and how I described it. Big words and exalted notions—along with everything else—fell away. I wrote notes to generous friends to ask for things that were needed: whole-grain bread for my father, tea, toilet paper. I wrote letters to Han and my beloved band of friends back at Gabriel Metsustraat, describing where I was, the utterly out-of-this-world but entirely in-this-world place where I'd arrived: the expanse of barracks stretching across the remote heath; the fields of lupine just beyond the barbed wire; the intricate and busy and class-driven society (even there) that existed within. I recorded sights that were enough to bring on weeping that if begun would never stop. A friend requested that I write in my style about Westerbork, and I did, in two long letters to people I had never met. As always, interior perspective permeated my descriptions.

You can see all this for yourself in the letters I wrote—a hundred faces and stories and moments that I tried to see without prejudice. I sat side by side with the journalist Philip Mechanicus and wrote about what I saw, right in front of us: a transport train being filled with two thousand of our fellow prisoners. By then I was no longer paralyzed by self-consciousness or grand notions of myself as a writer. My work was to bear witness. If I had any dream or ambition, it was to be the thinking heart of the barracks.

The historical times in which my life unfolded carry a weight and solemnity all their own. But your life is unfolding in historical times just as surely as mine did—times that are yours to reckon with as I did mine, striking your own balance between inner and outer realities. *Time is the fire in which we burn*—I always loved that line. Know yourself and know the particular and unique period in which you live, too.

When I was at Westerbork I thought a great deal about who would come after us, and what we could leave behind for them to build on. Don't we all want to leave something behind? Don't you? It was such a deep desire—for all our suffering not to have been in vain. I came to believe that what I could contribute was my refusal to add to the hatred, to add not one atom more of it to the crucible we were in. Perhaps that was my life's work, even more than writing. What do you call the work of not hating, the wish to be a balm for all wounds?

SUFFERING AND DEATH

WHEN I WAS YOUNGER I OFTEN BEMOANED THE
FACT THAT I HAD NOT EXPERIENCED LIFE IN THE
RAW; my comfortable upbringing, my pleasant life at
Han's, my stimulating work with Spier—I sometimes
doubted whether all my deep convictions held any
merit, having never been tested. Who was I to even
use the word *suffering* when it came to my life?

But I *did* suffer! We all do! I suffered in my mind,
in my body, for reasons great and small—when I
was depressed; when I was tormented by desire and
jealousy; when I witnessed acts of cruelty; when my
gut acted up and laid me low; when I couldn't find
the right words; when we were unable to stanch the
reign of hatred; when people I loved died; when I was
murdered …

The causes of my suffering changed, as did the
circumstances in which they arose. But over the
course of my life my understanding of suffering and
my response to it also changed, and that made all
the difference. Not all of a sudden, and not to the
exclusion of all moments of despair or misery, but
accepting it as a necessary and natural part of life and
of creativity helped me see that suffering can be borne;
it need not make us desperate. Reconciling myself to
suffering lifted some of its weight. It no longer felt like
the suffering I had known when all I wanted to do

was escape it. Accepted, it occupied a different place inside me, one that provoked less mental anguish and emotional response. It was the *idea* of suffering, rather than suffering itself, that needed to be destroyed. I became more interested in carrying what needed to be carried and letting it transform, as it inevitably did. In that process, I too was transformed.

What I am saying has nothing to do with resignation or defeatism, neither of which I harbored a drop of. There is such a thing, you know, as an active passivity, a detachment that is fully attentive and aware.

It was one of my prayers that we might all help each other bear our burdens together, wherever we find and however we define and experience cold and dark and hunger. Wherever we are, let us, as Rilke urges, belong and be there with all our hearts. We *all* suffer; suffering is without borders, a thing that connects us.

Death also connects us; we all die. For most of my life I had very little experience with death. Before killing wrapped itself around us like a shroud, I could count on one hand or two the number of people I had known who had died—two of my teachers, a childhood friend from Deventer, the bookseller who ran the Communist bookstore in Amsterdam.

You have your own tally, your own experience with death, so far. Have your encounters with it been up close or from far away, and where do you sit with it now?

In the end, the slice of history I lived my life in provided an overexposure to death. Said differently: it offered me intimate access. Not every period of history does that. But before I learned to live with its abiding presence and became intimately acquainted with it, I was just as removed and naïve as anyone else who has yet to encounter it.

When I was twenty-six, a former teacher of mine, Professor Bonger, committed suicide. He was my first encounter with someone taking death into his own hands, although he was certainly not the last. And in between his suicide and the many that followed, I came to my own reckoning with that particular way to die.

I saw Professor Bonger the night before he killed himself, the night that Holland capitulated to the Germans, May 15, 1940. I'd been gone from university for several years by then, but I recognized him instantly when I saw him walking by the skating club that evening. It was a profoundly sad night for so many of us; it felt to me as if our hearts were all beating together, a slow, labored pulse, now that the Germans had crushed our country's brief effort to hold them at bay, poor Rotterdam bombed to bits. Bonger was walking ahead of me, head down, smoking, emanating the same dark intensity he'd always brought to his lectures. I hurried a bit to catch up and called to him, *Professor.* He didn't know who I was at first, that was quite clear, and even after I'd provided the necessary reminders of which of his classes I had taken, his eyes flickered only a general recognition. But he offered a sad smile and indicated with a slight thrust of his chin that we might continue walking together. I instinctively linked my arm through his. It was bold to do so, but in the moment felt entirely natural. You see how that happens in times of national tragedy: strangers embracing, that instinctive need to turn to one another and hold on. What was happening in our country that night felt so grave and palpable. I took his arm and we walked together.

The news that he had put a bullet in his brain hours after we parted was initially impossible for me to take in. My friend Becker came by the apartment the next morning to tell me. *But I just spoke to him*, I kept saying, over and over, as if my having spoken to him the night before somehow guaranteed his existence, protected him. But of course there is no protection.

And Professor Bonger's despair over the Occupation had been fully evident: *They will eat us alive.* I should not have been as shocked as I was, as unable to comprehend, so insistent in my denial. But death is *always* sudden and irrevocable and stunning, and I had had so little experience with it up to that point.

In the years after Bonger's death, suicides increased as roundups began and resisters were hunted down. At Westerbork, suicides were a regular occurrence, most often before the weekly transports east were to depart from the camp. As a working member of the Jewish Council I witnessed the aftermath of a number of those deaths. I often thought of Professor Bonger and of how far I had come from the disbelief with which I'd responded to his suicide. The deaths at the camp deepened the unfathomable sadness we were already awash in, but they no longer occasioned disbelief.

I told you that I sometimes harbored thoughts of suicide when I was depressed, more from a sense of internal chaos than in response to external events. But I grew beyond the inclination to ever take my own life as my understanding and acceptance of suffering changed. Something I read in a letter written by a man named Walter Rathenau spoke deeply to me—I copied it twice into my diaries:

*This kind of death—and this is my deep
conviction—is not a liberation like a natural ending
for which we carry no responsibility. Every act of
violence has lasting aftereffects, as does everything
we do. We are here to take some of the world's
suffering upon ourselves by baring our breast to it,
not to increase it by our own violence. I know that
you suffer, and I suffer with you. Be kind to that
suffering, and it will be kind to you. It is increased
by desire and by indignation; gentleness lulls it to
sleep like a child. You have so much love in you;
devote it all to your fellow men, to children, to
things, even to yourself and your pain. Do not be
lonely; do not allow that; surmount that obstacle,
look it in the eye ...*

Some consider my refusal to hide from the Nazis and
my request to be sent to work at Westerbork a form of
suicide. But I disagree. I did not give up on life; it was
taken from me, by a system permeated with hatred.
I *wanted* life, oh I did, but not at the cost of holding
myself separate from others of whom I was a part.

At Westerbork, where circumstances were grim and
the future a looming tragedy, where the option of
suicide made a perfect kind of sense, I loved and
treasured life absolutely.

I needn't have worried about being tested. We all are, at various times in our lives, given opportunities to enact what we have cultivated in our deepest selves. Some tests are extreme and public and devastating, and others so quiet and nuanced that you may be the only one to know you are facing a fundamental juncture. Each step matters. Nothing—no gesture or action or thought—is ever wasted.

There was another important death in my life that I have not spoken of yet—a death unto itself, but then, isn't every death? Spier died. Spier died, he did, in 1942, of lung cancer, the night before the Gestapo came to arrest him. I collapsed when I heard the news, even though I'd known his death was imminent. There is no evading the shock of death, or grief. But I knew by then how to carry someone inside me, regardless of physical separation.

Even before Spier died, I had made my decision to go to Westerbork and face whatever life held for me on my own. Death did not silence his voice in me or my sense of his presence. I felt no need for photographs or keepsakes, or even to say his name. Rilke—someone else I carried inside me—reminded me:

> For this *is wrong, if anything is wrong:*
> *not to enlarge the freedom of a love*

with all the inner freedom one can summon.
We need, in love, to practice only this:
letting each other go. For holding on
comes easily; we do not need to learn it.

Do you think it's possible to prepare for death—your own, or the deaths of those you love? Maybe death seems unimaginably far away. For the last years of my life I lived with it close by; before we even knew Spier was ill, before I went to Westerbork, death had already crossed a threshold into my life. It entered with my understanding that the Nazis meant to kill us all. Letting go of any illusions about that crystallized something in me, and allowed death to take up residence; I accepted it. I came to believe that how I died, although I did not *want* to die, would show me who I really was. My personal fate was not paramount to me, and I was firm in my conviction to share the fate of my people. Living with death enlarged and enriched my life and made a difference in how I lived it.

I've told you about others' deaths. Perhaps there is something I can tell you about myself as I came very close to my own. I did not wonder about any afterlife so much as what life would be like for those who survived. I knew there would be need for a reckoning: the terror and horror we had unleashed on our poor world demanded that. I didn't want those who survived and those who were born into new generations to have to start from scratch, as if none of us had held on to beauty and love. I wanted those who survived to inherit a world with some foundations still standing. I wanted people to know that we kept God alive during the times we lived through.

I can also tell you that as close as I lived to imminent death at Westerbork, as accepting as I was of death as an inevitable and necessary part of life, in the moment of receiving news that I was to be put on transport east, my legs buckled. Just as they had when I received the news of Spier's death. I fell down—different from the many times I'd fallen on my knees to pray. Or maybe not; maybe that collapse was my ultimate prayer. No matter how close to death I'd been living, knowing my time was near, it still overwhelmed me, if only in the moment. Bowing to the hugeness of it all.

I came back to my deepest self, though—what comfort there always is in that homecoming— came back as I'd done a thousand times over the course of my months at Westerbork, and in the years before, too. Others, and other things, filled my consciousness—my mother and father and brother were on the list for transport as well. There were many tasks to attend to in preparation for departure—tasks I had done for countless others whose names had appeared on the list before mine did. I was prepared, having returned to the solid center within me. I had practiced turning wholly inward many times, and the turning I knew well served me well.

GOD

I BELIEVE IN GOD AND I BELIEVE IN MAN.

I hope that is implicit in everything I have written.
But even for me, who proclaimed in my journal with
such conviction, *One must have the courage to speak
God's name*, it is hardly a simple thing to do. I know
how it can sound, that word, *God*, landing on your
ears. I know it can boomerang, spark instant and
needless divisions. What do any of us even mean
when we say it?

And how, though it permeates everything, all that
I have been saying to you, can I possibly talk *about*
God? It's not faith I lack—once God came to me and
I to God, faith took hold and rapidly grew. It's the
utter insufficiency of words that constrains me.

My dear friend Tide confided her every wish to an
almighty God she believed capable of dispensing happy
endings; I sometimes found her notion annoyingly
childish, even as I harbored notions of my own—a
God whom *we* must help, a God it is incumbent upon
us to keep alive. I never believed in a God who was
somehow responsible for us or what was happening
in the world. I always believed that each one of us is
responsible both for the suffering we inflict on one
another and for alleviating it. The God to whom I held
myself accountable was not accountable to me.

I promised to always be a dwelling place for God and to seek out dwellings in others; to trust God, whatever the circumstances, and to accept whatever came. Of course I had my preferences—even when it came to suffering—but in the end, they too had to be let go of. *Not my will, but thine.* Over time my inclination to disparage other people's conceptions of God, even silently, went away. No idea of God is God. Not mine, not yours.

Rilke's words probably come closest to capturing what I came to know: *through every being single space extends: / outer space within.* The spaciousness that grew in me had room enough for all contradictions, destruction and creation, God and death, beauty and terror. No wonder I sometimes felt I could hold all of history inside me.

And paradox abounded! I experienced great abundance even as material scarcity set in; I felt entirely free when I was ostensibly a prisoner; my spirit grew lighter and brighter even as my physical state deteriorated. My internal environment created its own weather, unburdened by external conditions.

I can't know what, if anything, the word *God* evokes in you—your notion of what or if God is, or is not. Perhaps we should talk about intimacy instead, or the great, encompassing wave, or the Longing that cannot be satisfied by small satisfactions—are these designations any better? Finally, all conceptions and descriptions fall short and fall away, while that which is more than, deeper than, within and beyond, too, remains. Acknowledging the impossibility of naming or containing it, why *not*, then, call it God—a word I once found unnecessary and could barely write without the qualification of quotation marks. But I needed *something*—a word, a metaphor—for what I was encountering in the depths of myself.

And for a while this simple definition seemed to suffice: God was just another name for the deepest part of myself. Everything kept expanding, though—both my relationship with God and my attempts to articulate it. I discovered a deep well inside me, and in that well, sometimes buried beneath all kinds of blockage, but there for the digging, always and still: God. Soon even the images of resting places expanded—dwellings, houses, the arms of God—metaphors that tried, impossibly, to convey myself as both container and contained. By the end, it was not enough only to declare the name or locate God within me; I was compelled to search God out in every person I met, to clear the path for God to them, and them to God. Eventually I entered into an uninterrupted dialogue with God that became my deepest reality and source of sustenance. It was a great and continuous evolution.

I worked at deepening my spiritual life, and in turn, my spiritual deepening worked on me. Practice was essential, just as it is in writing or any discipline. I became more attentive to how I thought and behaved, more serious about my relationships, trying not to underestimate the power of petty grievances and the damage they can do. Prayer concentrated me. Even a few minutes given over to meditation left their mark. I turned inward again and again. When I drifted off, let my moods or circumstance consume me, I was always left diminished, and I returned, drawn back to the relationship that genuinely nourished me and connected me to all others. That we are made in God's image and likeness both heartened and sometimes confounded me; we reflect and lead each other to God.

In Westerbork, even the precondition of having to know people before I could love them fell away. That he or she was a fellow human being was enough. What did it matter where they came from or how they chewed their food? Love itself mattered more than the objects of my love, just as how we bear our burdens matters more than whatever those burdens are.

I am remembering, now, the beloved tree that grew outside my bedroom window in Amsterdam, all the beautiful nighttime silhouettes it bestowed upon me. One day it was unceremoniously de-limbed by city workers. I was afraid to face its sad remains that night, so sure of its ruin. Instead I discovered that what was left was beautiful, too, beauty in a new form that I could love just as well. My capacity for loving grew as the particulars of who or what I loved became less and less important. Love itself got the upper hand.

I told you, sad girls, I would talk about love. That's what I came to. And I always wanted to pass along what I held firm to in my short life. Toward the end, it was I who expressed the perhaps childish notion that love was the only hope for our world. I knew it was asking a great deal, perhaps even too much, to hold on to love in a time of such enormous suffering, but I asked it all the same, and tried to live accordingly. You hold on, too—all of us joined together in carrying our burdens, God in me and God in you.

Biographical Note

Etty Hillesum was born in Middelburg, Holland, in 1914, grew up in Deventer, and attended university in Amsterdam, where she completed a degree in law. She also studied Slavic languages and tutored students in Russian while living as the housekeeper in the home of Han Wegerif. In 1941 she started therapy with the analyst Julius Spier and soon began keeping a diary to explore her psychological and spiritual development. That development became the primary focus and undergirding foundation of her life.

In 1942 the Nazi occupation of Holland intensified its prohibitions against Jews, including roundups and orders to report to Camp Westerbork in Drenthe Province, northeastern Netherlands. Originally established by the Dutch government as a refugee center for Jews who had illegally entered the country, Westerbork became, in 1942, a transit camp run by German security police through which Jews were transported to concentration camps in Poland. Shortly after securing a job at the Jewish Council, Etty asked to be sent to work at Westerbork, where she felt she could be of use in the Department of Social Welfare for People in Transit. Due to illness, she spent nearly half of the next ten months back in Amsterdam, returning to Westerbork whenever she was able. In June 1943 she returned to the camp for the final time. In July the Jewish Council was disbanded, and she became an official Westerbork internee. In September, Etty, along with her mother, her father, her brother Mischa, and two thousand others, was put on transport to Auschwitz-Birkenau. She was murdered there, in November 1943. In all, over one hundred thousand Jews passed through Westerbork before being sent, via weekly transports, to concentration camps.

In 1981, an abridged volume of Etty Hillesum's diaries from 1941 and 1942 was published in Holland. The English translation, *An Interrupted Life*, was published in 1983 (along with many other foreign editions), to widespread international acclaim. Letters she wrote during her time at the camp were also published, in a book entitled *Letters from Westerbork*.

Author's Note

For Sad Girls is intended as an introduction to Etty Hillesum and an invitation to read her own words, all of them, for yourself.

Nearly everything in *For Sad Girls* is drawn from what Etty Hillesum wrote. Some phrases are exactly hers, many more are paraphrased; except for the framing conceit of her speaking retrospectively to sad girls, and my overarching interpretation of her diaries, very little is imagined. Everything is meant to be an arrow pointing back to her.

Sources

Various editions of Etty Hillesum's works, including *An Interrupted Life* and *Letters from Westerbork*, are available from booksellers.

Etty: The Letters and Diaries of Etty Hillesum, 1941–1943, edited by Klaas A. D. Smelik (Eerdmans Publishing Company, 2002), is a complete, unabridged, richly annotated resource; it is the version I drew from in writing *For Sad Girls*.

There is also a two-volume bilingual (Dutch and English), unabridged, annotated edition of her work: *Etty Hillesum: The Complete Works, 1941–1943*, edited by Klaas A. D. Smelik and Meins G. S. Coetsier (Shaker Verlag, 2014).

The website of the Etty Hillesum Research Center, www.ehoc.nl, is a fine source for the ongoing and wide-ranging scholarly work on Etty Hillesum, with news of conferences and publications. Included in the Center's listing of books and articles about Etty Hillesum are many that deepened and shaped my understanding of her. Two essays specifically informed this book:

Siertsema, Bettine, "New Light on Etty Hillesum's Actions in Camp Westerbork," in *The Lasting Significance of Etty*

Hillesum's Writings: Proceedings of the Third International Etty Hillesum Conference at Middelburg, September 2018, edited by Klaas A. D. Smelik (Amsterdam University Press, *2019*), pp. 341–351.

Smelik, Klaas A. D., "Romance Down by the River IJssel: The First Meeting Between Etty Hillesum and Klaas Smelik Senior," in *Reading Etty Hillesum in Context: Writings, Life, and Influences of a Visionary Author*, edited by Klaas A. D. Smelik, Gerrit Van Oord, and Jurjen Wiersma (Amsterdam University Press, 2018), pp. 259–271.

Philip Mechanicus's account of his time at Westerbork, *Year of Fear: A Jewish Prisoner Waits for Auschwitz*, translated from the Dutch by Irene S. Gibbons (Hawthorn Books, 1964), provided another perspective of that time and place.

I highly recommend Carol Lee Flinder's excellent monograph, *Becoming Etty: The Brief, Incandescent Life of Etty Hillesum* (available on Kindle). It was originally published as a chapter, "The Thinking Heart of the Barracks," in the book *Enduring Lives: Portraits of Women of Faith in Action*, by Carol Lee Flinders (Orbis Books, 2012).

The generous and insightful interviews contained in *Conversations with Biographical Novelists: Truthful Fictions Across the Globe*, edited by Michael Lackey (Bloomsbury Academic, 2018), helped me envision a way to present Etty Hillesum's life.

The Rilke quotation on pages 79–80 is from "Requiem for a Friend," in *The Selected Poetry of Rainer Maria Rilke*, edited and translated by Stephen Mitchell (Random House, 1980), p. 85.

The Rathenau quotation on page 78 appears in *Etty: The Letters and Diaries of Etty Hillesum, 1941–1943*, edited by Klaas A. D. Smelik (Eerdmans Publishing Company, 2002), p. 132.

Acknowledgments

Special thanks to Klaas A. D. Smelik, who has
done so much to make known the life and work
of Etty Hillesum, and to Denise de Costa, writer
and scholar and my dear Dutch sister. Thank you
to all the scholars around the world whose work
on Etty Hillesum has informed and broadened my
understanding of her. Thank you to Steven Holt, true
friend and trusted reader, and to Gail O'Donnell,
RSCJ, who believed in this book.

I am also grateful for a 2011 residency at Hedgebrook
during which I worked with this material.

So many people encouraged, supported, and
nourished me over the many years I worked to find a
way to write about Etty Hillesum. I thank them all.

Made in the USA
Monee, IL
22 December 2020